CONTENT

D1569103

1.   **SECTION 1:** Defining Polymathy

11.   **Section 2:** Becoming a Polymath

23.   **Section 3:** Identifying as a Polymath

43.   **Section 4:** Polymathic Skills

61.   **Section 5:** Professional Life

73.   **Section 6:** Social Aspects of My Polymathy

87.   **Section 7:** The Emotions of Polymathy

101.   **Section 8:** Resources & Support

113.   **Section 9:** My Legacy

126.   **Section 10:** Free Space for Other Thoughts

A NOTE FROM THE AUTHOR

Polymathic people have broad expertise, exposure, and experiences across disciplines. They do not occupy the narrow boxes society prescribes. Polymathic people are curious rebels, lifelong and self-directed learners who experience challenges and joys from living life on their own terms. They are also frequently misunderstood and underappreciated. Though a polymath has great strengths and joys, polymaths may also experience challenges.

My hope is that you will use this journal as a tool to help you support your journey towards your fullest and most authentic expression of yourself. May your life be your greatest masterpiece.

With my support,

Angela

■ Dr. Angela Cotellessa

SECTION 1

Defining Polymathy

1

"You don't become what you want, you become what you believe."

~Oprah Winfrey

To me, being a polymath means:

_____

_____

_____

_____

_____

_____

_____

_____

_____

_____

_____

_____

_____

_____

_____

_____

_____

_____

_____

_____

2

"The only person you are destined to become is the person you decide to be."

~Ralph Waldo Emerson

Evidence of my own polymathic nature includes:

_____

_____

_____

_____

_____

_____

_____

_____

_____

_____

_____

_____

_____

_____

_____

_____

_____

_____

_____

_____

_____

_____

3

"Do not yearn to be popular; be exquisite. Do not desire to be famous; be loved. Do not take pride in being expected; be palpable, unmistakable."

~C. JoyBell C.

Polymaths embrace their unique "onlyness."
Here are the ways in which I am a true original:

_____

_____

_____

_____

_____

_____

_____

_____

_____

_____

_____

_____

_____

_____

_____

_____

_____

_____

_____

_____

4

"In the social jungle of human existence, there is no feeling of being alive without a sense of identity."

~**Erik Erikson**

Polymaths exist on a spectrum. At the far end are eminent creative geniuses, and on the other end are people who may be curious about multiple fields but do not actually pursue them in any depth. Where on this spectrum do you believe you fall? Place an "X" where you think you are on the spectrum, and explain your rationale in the space below.

←——————————————————————————→

I'm not really that polymathic much at all

I'm an eminent creative genius!

_____

_____

_____

_____

_____

_____

_____

_____

_____

_____

_____

_____

_____

_____

SECTION 2

Becoming a Polymath

1

"May all your trails be crooked, winding, lonesome, dangerous, leading to the most amazing view... where something strange and more beautiful and more full of wonder than your deepest dreams waits for you."

~Edward Abbey

I first realized I was polymathic when:

_____

_____

_____

_____

_____

_____

_____

_____

_____

_____

_____

_____

_____

_____

_____

_____

_____

_____

_____

_____

2

"I am my own experiment. I am my own work of art."

~Madonna

Elements of and experiences in my childhood that
helped promote my polymathic development were:

_____

_____

_____

_____

_____

_____

_____

_____

_____

_____

_____

_____

_____

_____

_____

_____

_____

_____

_____

_____

_____

3

"One can have no smaller or greater mastery than mastery of oneself."

~Leonardo da Vinci

I must live my life in a polymathic way because:

_____

_____

_____

_____

_____

_____

_____

_____

_____

_____

_____

_____

_____

_____

_____

_____

_____

_____

_____

_____

4

"To develop a complete mind: Study the art of science; study the science of art. Learn how to see. Realize that everything connects to everything else."

~Leonardo da Vinci

If I could go back in time and tell my younger self anything about becoming a polymath, this is what I would say:

_____

_____

_____

_____

_____

_____

_____

_____

_____

_____

_____

_____

_____

_____

_____

_____

_____

_____

_____

_____

_____

5

"The purpose of life, after all, is to live it, to taste experience to the utmost, to reach out eagerly and without fear for newer and richer experience."

~**Eleanor Roosevelt**

Polymathy has been described as a way of being "all in" at life itself. In what ways do you show you are committed to having the full human experience?

_____

_____

_____

_____

_____

_____

_____

_____

_____

_____

_____

_____

_____

_____

_____

_____

_____

_____

_____

_____

_____

_____

_____

SECTION 3

Identifying as a Polymath

1

"I have no special talent. I am only passionately curious."

~Albert Einstein

The word(s) I like to use to describe my own polymathy are:

_____

_____

_____

_____

_____

_____

_____

_____

_____

The reason I like these word(s) is because:

_____

_____

_____

_____

_____

_____

_____

_____

_____

_____

_____

2

"What we choose, we become."

~Jason Silva

If my own polymathy had a logo, that image (or my brand) would look like this:

3

"The most adventurous journey
to embark on is the journey to
yourself. The most exciting thing
to discover is who you really are.
The most treasured pieces that you
can find are all the pieces of you.
The most special portrait you can
recognize is the portrait of your
soul."

~C. JoyBell C.

No matter what people say, I know that being a polymath is right for me because:

_____

_____

_____

_____

_____

_____

_____

_____

_____

_____

_____

_____

_____

_____

_____

_____

_____

_____

_____

_____

4

"I think everything in life is art. What you do. How you dress. The way you love someone, and how you talk. Your smile and your personality. What you believe in, and all your dreams. The way you drink your tea. How you decorate your home. Or party. Your grocery list. The food you make. How your writing looks. And the way you feel. Life is art."

~Helena Bonham Carter

The thing I enjoy most about being a polymath is:

_____

_____

_____

_____

_____

_____

_____

_____

_____

_____

_____

_____

_____

_____

_____

_____

_____

_____

5

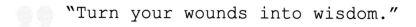

"Turn your wounds into wisdom."

~Oprah Winfrey

The hardest aspect of my polymathy is:

_____

_____

_____

_____

_____

_____

_____

_____

_____

_____

_____

_____

_____

_____

_____

_____

_____

_____

_____

6

"There's power in allowing yourself to be known and heard, in owning your unique story, in using your authentic voice."

~Michelle Obama

If I had/did/experienced _____, it would help me embrace my polymathic identity even more. Here's why:

_____

_____

_____

_____

_____

_____

_____

_____

_____

_____

_____

_____

_____

_____

_____

_____

_____

_____

_____

_____

7

"Live as if you were to die tomorrow. Learn as if you were to live forever."

~Mahatma Gandhi

I appreciate polymathic living because:

_____

_____

_____

_____

_____

_____

_____

_____

_____

_____

_____

_____

_____

_____

_____

_____

_____

_____

_____

_____

_____

8

"I don't want to get to the end of my life and find that I lived just the length of it. I want to have lived the width of it as well."

~David Ackerman

Polymathic people may have many selves within their one "self." Here are the different versions of me that exist within my individual personhood:

_____

_____

_____

_____

_____

_____

_____

_____

_____

_____

_____

_____

_____

_____

_____

_____

_____

_____

_____

9

"Do I contradict myself? Very well, then, I contradict myself; I am large -- I contain multitudes."

~Walt Whitman

For some people, polymathy may mean having contradictory or surprising elements of their personhood, beliefs, or background; in my case, those elements are:

I am this....   *...at the same time that I am also this*

_____   _____

_____   _____

_____   _____

_____   _____

_____   _____

_____   _____

_____   _____

_____   _____

_____   _____

_____   _____

_____   _____

_____   _____

_____   _____

_____   _____

_____   _____

_____   _____

_____   _____

SECTION 4

Polymathic Skills

1

"A human being should be able to change a diaper, plan an invasion, butcher a hog, conn a ship, design a building, write a sonnet, balance accounts, build a wall, set a bone, comfort the dying, take orders, give orders, cooperate, act alone, solve equations, analyze a new problem, pitch manure, program a computer, cook a tasty meal, fight efficiently, die gallantly. Specialization is for insects."

~**Robert A. Heinlein**

A hallmark of polymaths is that they enjoy continual, self-directed, lifelong learning. I love learning because:

_____

_____

_____

_____

_____

_____

_____

_____

_____

_____

_____

_____

_____

_____

_____

_____

_____

_____

_____

2

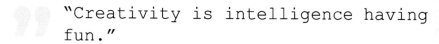

"Creativity is intelligence having fun."

~**Albert Einstein**

My greatest polymathic superpower is:

_____

_____

_____

_____

_____

_____

_____

_____

_____

_____

_____

_____

_____

_____

_____

_____

_____

_____

_____

3

"Anything that you learn becomes your wealth, a wealth that cannot be taken away from you; whether you learn it in a building called school or in the school of life. To learn something new is a timeless pleasure and a valuable treasure. And not all things that you learn are taught to you, but many things that you learn you realize you have taught yourself."

~**C. JoyBell C.**

Polymaths are continual learners. What is your favorite way to learn new information?

_____

_____

_____

_____

_____

_____

_____

_____

_____

_____

_____

_____

_____

_____

_____

_____

_____

_____

4

"It had long since come to my attention that people of accomplishment rarely sat back and let things happen to them. They went out and happened to things."

~Leonardo da Vinci

Because polymaths have expertise and experience across different disciplines, they are in a unique position to creatively innovate. What sorts of unique combinations or creative insights have been or could be possible because of your unique make-up?

_____

_____

_____

_____

_____

_____

_____

_____

_____

_____

_____

_____

_____

_____

_____

_____

_____

_____

5

"Don't fear failure. Not failure, but low aim, is the crime. In great attempts it is glorious even to fail."

~Bruce Lee

The various hobbies I have enjoyed over the years are:

_____

_____

_____

_____

_____

_____

_____

_____

_____

_____

Future hobbies I hope to explore are:

_____

_____

_____

_____

_____

_____

_____

_____

_____

6

"Be yourself; everyone else is already taken."

~**Leonardo da Vinci**

Polymaths are intra-personally diverse individuals. What types of diversity do you have within yourself?

_____

_____

_____

_____

_____

_____

_____

_____

_____

_____

_____

_____

_____

_____

_____

_____

_____

_____

_____

_____

7

"Some people live in cages with bars built from their own fears and doubts. Some people live in cages with bars built from other people's fears and doubts; their parents, their friends, their brothers and sisters, their families. Some people live in cages with bars built from the choices others made for them, the circumstances other people imposed upon them. And some people break free."

~C. JoyBell C.

Polymaths express self-leadership as they self-author and curate their own life stories. I've expressed self-leadership when I:

_____

_____

_____

_____

_____

_____

_____

_____

_____

_____

_____

_____

_____

_____

_____

_____

_____

_____

7

"I am not a genius. I'm just a tremendous bundle of experience."

~R. Buckminster Fuller

Polymaths must juggle many interests and commitments, and manage their time. Here's how I manage my multiple interests and pursuits:

_____

_____

_____

_____

_____

_____

_____

_____

_____

_____

_____

_____

_____

_____

_____

_____

_____

_____

_____

SECTION 5

Professional Life

1

"Formal education will make you a living; self-education will make you a fortune."

~**Jim Rohn**

We live in an age of specialization, where the dominant ideology says that to be successful, you must specialize very narrowly professionally. Do you agree with this approach in your own life? Why or why not?

_____

_____

_____

_____

_____

_____

_____

_____

_____

_____

_____

_____

_____

_____

_____

_____

_____

_____

_____

2

"Whatever you are, be a good one."

~**Abraham Lincoln**

At work, this is how my polymathy is (or is not) leveraged:

_____

_____

_____

_____

_____

_____

_____

_____

_____

_____

_____

_____

_____

_____

_____

_____

_____

_____

_____

3

"There is no greater agony than bearing an untold story inside you."

~Maya Angelou

Organizations frequently do not know how to support polymathic people. What do you wish organizations did differently to support polymathic people?

_____

_____

_____

_____

_____

_____

_____

_____

_____

_____

_____

_____

_____

_____

_____

_____

_____

4

"Do what you can, with what you have, where you are."

~**Theodore Roosevelt**

Polymathy impacts one's finances, and finances impact one's polymathy. Here's how those concepts relate and show up in my life:

_____

_____

_____

_____

_____

_____

_____

_____

_____

_____

_____

_____

_____

_____

_____

_____

_____

_____

5

"It doesn't make sense to hire smart people and then tell them what to do; we hire smart people so they can tell us what to do."

~Steve Jobs

My ideal professional life looks like this:

_____

_____

_____

_____

_____

_____

_____

_____

_____

_____

_____

_____

_____

_____

_____

_____

_____

_____

SECTION 6

Social Aspects of
My Polymathy

1

"You have so many extraordinary gifts; how can you expect to live an ordinary life?"

~Louisa May Alcott

This is how I explain my polymathic nature to others:

_____

_____

_____

_____

_____

_____

_____

_____

_____

_____

_____

_____

_____

_____

_____

_____

_____

_____

2

"Listen to the mustn'ts, child. Listen to the don'ts. Listen to the shouldn'ts, the impossibles, the won'ts. Listen to the never haves, then listen close to me... Anything can happen, child. Anything can be."

~Shel Silverstein

Sometimes, people seem very critical of other people's polymathic nature. Those people are:

_____

_____

_____

_____

_____

_____

_____

_____

Here is how I plan to deal with their negative comments that may be said to me about the way I live my life:

_____

_____

_____

_____

_____

_____

_____

_____

_____

_____

3

"You can't live your life for other people. You've got to do what's right for you, even if it hurts some people you love."

~Nicholas Sparks, The Notebook

If I could help others to understand one thing about my polymathy, the most important thing I would want them to know is that:

_____

_____

_____

_____

_____

_____

_____

_____

_____

_____

_____

_____

_____

_____

_____

_____

_____

_____

4

"The delicate balance of mentoring someone is not creating them in your own image, but giving them the opportunity to create themselves."

~**Steven Spielberg**

A polymath I look up to is

_____ and this is why:

_____

_____

_____

_____

_____

_____

_____

_____

_____

_____

_____

_____

_____

_____

_____

_____

_____

5

"Be supportive of others the way you would want them to be supportive of you."

~Ken Poirot

I can help other people explore their polymathy by:

_____

_____

_____

_____

_____

_____

_____

_____

_____

_____

_____

_____

_____

_____

_____

_____

_____

_____

_____

6

"The purpose of man is to live, not to exist."

~Jack London

When people think of me, I hope they think:

_____

_____

_____

_____

_____

_____

_____

_____

_____

_____

_____

_____

_____

_____

_____

_____

_____

_____

_____

SECTION 7

The Emotions of Polymathy

1

"When one door of happiness closes, another opens; but often we look so long at the closed door that we do not see the one which has been opened for us."

~Helen Keller

Being a polymathic person is not necessarily easy. When I have experienced challenges along my polymathic journey, here is how I have navigated those challenges:

_____

_____

_____

_____

_____

_____

_____

_____

_____

_____

_____

_____

_____

_____

_____

_____

_____

_____

2

"I can't give you a sure-fire formula for success, but I can give you a formula for failure: try to please everybody all the time."

~**Herbert Bayard Swope**

The biggest misunderstanding people have of my polymathic
nature is:

_____

_____

_____

_____

_____

_____

_____

_____

_____

_____

_____

_____

_____

_____

_____

_____

_____

_____

_____

_____

3

"What does it mean if I'm afraid?
Does it mean something bad is
going to happen?" "No, it doesn't
mean something bad is going to
happen. It just means that you
have the chance to be brave."

~C. JoyBell C.

Being a polymath requires bravery to forge your own unique path. In what ways have you shown bravery along your life path?

_____

_____

_____

_____

_____

_____

_____

_____

_____

_____

_____

_____

_____

_____

_____

_____

_____

_____

_____

_____

_____

4

"Do not go where the path may lead, go instead where there is no path and leave a trail."

~Ralph Waldo Emerson

Being a polymath requires a bit of rebelliousness—a refusal
to follow the standard prescription of how someone should
live their life. In what ways have you expressed rebelliousness
along your life journey so far?

_____

_____

_____

_____

_____

_____

_____

_____

_____

_____

_____

_____

_____

_____

_____

_____

_____

5

"You're the author of your life's story. You can start a new chapter anytime you choose."

~**Amy Atherton**

The world is a place full of possibility. The thing that excites me the most about my future as a polymath is:

_____

_____

_____

_____

_____

_____

_____

_____

_____

_____

_____

_____

_____

_____

_____

_____

_____

6

"If my life is going to mean anything, I have to live it myself."

~**Rick Riordan, The Lightning Thief**

When I look back upon my journey as a polymath so far, the thing I'm most proud of is:

_____

_____

_____

_____

_____

_____

_____

_____

_____

_____

_____

_____

_____

_____

_____

_____

_____

_____

SECTION 8

Resources & Support

1

"Surround yourself with only people who are going to lift you higher."

~Oprah Winfrey

The people who support me being my authentic, full self are:

_____

_____

_____

_____

_____

_____

_____

Here's how I know they support me in all my dimensions:

_____

_____

_____

_____

_____

_____

_____

_____

_____

2

"Always bear in mind that your own resolution to succeed is more important than any one thing."

~**Abraham Lincoln**

The tools that help me pursue my polymathy are:

_____

_____

_____

_____

_____

_____

_____

_____

_____

_____

_____

_____

_____

_____

_____

_____

_____

_____

_____

3

"Look closely at the present you
are constructing. It should look
like the future you are dreaming."

~Alice Walker

When I have many interests and projects, the way I determine which to focus on next is:

_____

_____

_____

_____

_____

_____

_____

_____

_____

_____

_____

_____

_____

_____

_____

_____

_____

_____

_____

_____

4

"The best way to predict the future is to create it."

~**Abraham Lincoln**

In a nutshell, here's how I'd describe my life today:

_____

_____

_____

_____

_____

_____

Here's how I'd like my life to look in 1/5/10 years

_____

_____

_____

_____

_____

_____

Here are some action steps I can begin taking to get the life of my dreams:

_____

_____

_____

_____

_____

_____

5

"One can choose to go back toward safety or forward toward growth. Growth must be chosen again and again; fear must be overcome again and again."

~Abraham Maslow

These are the obstacles preventing me from experiencing my
fullest potential:

_____

_____

_____

_____

_____

_____

_____

_____

_____

And some strategies I can implement in the future to
overcome those obstacles are:

_____

_____

_____

_____

_____

_____

_____

_____

_____

_____

_____

SECTION 9

My Legacy

1

"To live is the rarest thing in the world. Most people just exist."

~Oscar Wilde

When you look back upon your life journey so far, what are
you most proud of?

_____

_____

_____

_____

_____

_____

_____

_____

_____

_____

_____

_____

_____

_____

_____

_____

_____

_____

_____

_____

2

"It is never too late to be what you might have been."

~George Eliot

Self-actualization, or reaching my highest potential, looks like this to me:

_____

_____

_____

_____

_____

_____

_____

_____

_____

_____

_____

_____

_____

_____

_____

_____

_____

_____

_____

_____

3

"Life isn't about finding yourself.
Life is about creating yourself."

~George Bernard Shaw

In order to be my best self, these are some of the things I would like to do/be/express/experience:

_____

_____

_____

_____

_____

_____

_____

_____

_____

_____

_____

_____

_____

_____

_____

_____

_____

_____

_____

_____

_____

4

"The human race is challenged more than ever before to demonstrate our mastery – not over nature but of ourselves."

~**Rachel Carson**

My polymathy helps me be my best self because:

_____

_____

_____

_____

_____

_____

_____

_____

_____

_____

_____

_____

_____

_____

_____

_____

_____

_____

_____

_____

5

"It is not the critic who counts; not the man who points out how the strong man stumbles, or where the doer of deeds could have done them better. The credit belongs to the man who is actually in the arena, whose face is marred by dust and sweat and blood; who strives valiantly; who errs, who comes short again and again, because there is no effort without error and shortcoming; but who does actually strive to do the deeds; who knows great enthusiasms, the great devotions; who spends himself in a worthy cause; who at the best knows in the end the triumph of high achievement, and who at the worst, if he fails, at least fails while daring greatly, so that his place shall never be with those whose cold and timid souls who neither know victory nor defeat."

~Theodore Roosevelt

Some ways in which I hope to contribute to society, my community, my family, friends, or profession during my lifetime are:

_____

_____

_____

_____

_____

_____

_____

_____

_____

_____

_____

_____

_____

_____

_____

_____

_____

_____

_____

_____

6

"The biggest adventure you can ever take is to live the life of your dreams."

~Oprah Winfrey

Near the end of my life, when I look back on how I lived it all, I will be proud to say this about how I did:

_____

_____

_____

_____

_____

_____

_____

_____

_____

_____

_____

_____

_____

_____

_____

_____

_____

_____

_____

_____

_____

SECTION 10

Free Space for
Other Thoughts

Made in the USA
Middletown, DE
27 March 2023